Something Big Has Been Here

Something BIG

Has Been Here

poems by JACK PRELUTSKY

drawings by JAMES STEVENSON

 Greenwillow Books, New York

First Edition

15 14 13 12 11 10 9 8 7 6 5 4 3 2 1

Library of Congress Cataloging-in-Publication Data
Prelutsky, Jack.
Something big has been here / Jack Prelutsky.
p.   cm.
Summary: An illustrated collection of humorous
poems on a variety of topics.
ISBN 0-688-06434-5.
1. Children's poetry, American.   [1. American poetry.
2. Humorous poetry.]   I. Stevenson, James (date) ill.
II Title.   PS3566.R36S66   1990
811'.54—dc20   89-34773   CIP   AC

To children's booksellers everywhere

Something Big Has Been Here

Something big has been here,
what it was, I do not know,
for I did not see it coming,
and I did not see it go,
but I hope I never meet it,
if I do, I'm in a fix,
for it left behind its footprints,
they are size nine-fifty-six.

An Early Worm Got out of Bed

An early worm got out of bed
and murmured, "I feel mean!
I'll put my darkest glasses on,
I'll paint myself bright green.

"I'll dress up in my wildest wig,
the one with purple bangs,
I'll also wear a pair of horns
and artificial fangs."

That early worm poked up its head,
which looked a perfect fright,
an early bird observed that worm
and lost its appetite.

I Know All the Sounds that the Animals Make

I know all the sounds that the animals make,
and make them all day from the moment I wake,
I roar like a mouse and I purr like a moose,
I hoot like a duck and I moo like a goose.

I squeak like a cat and I quack like a frog,
I oink like a bear and I honk like a hog,
I croak like a cow and I bark like a bee,
no wonder the animals marvel at me.

Happy Birthday, Mother Dearest

Happy birthday, Mother dearest,
we made breakfast just for you,
a watermelon omelette,
and a dish of popcorn too,
a cup of milk and sugar,
and a slice of blackened toast,
happy birthday, Mother dearest,
you're the one we love the most.

We're Four Ferocious Tigers

We're four ferocious tigers,
at least, that's what we seem,
our claws are at the ready,
our sharp incisors gleam,
we're quite intimidating,
our stare will make you blink,
our roar will make you shiver,
at least, that's what we think.

We're four ferocious tigers,
at least, that's what we hear,
our ominous demeanor
will chill your atmosphere,
and yet you need not fear us,
don't scream and run away,
we only eat spaghetti,
at least, that's what we say.

I Am Growing a Glorious Garden

I am growing a glorious garden,
resplendent with trumpets and flutes,
I am pruning euphonium bushes,
I am watering piccolo shoots,
my tubas and tambourines flourish,
surrounded by saxophone reeds,
I am planting trombones and pianos,
and sowing sweet sousaphone seeds.

I have cymbals galore in my garden,
staid oboes in orderly rows,
there are flowering fifes and violas
in the glade where the glockenspiel grows,
there are gongs and guitars in abundance,
there are violins high on the vine,
and an arbor of harps by the bower
where the cellos and clarinets twine.

My bassoons are beginning to blossom,
as my zithers and mandolins bloom,
my castanets happily chatter,
my kettledrums merrily boom,
the banjos that branch by the bugles
play counterpoint with a kazoo,
come visit my glorious garden
and hear it play music for you.

As Soon as Fred Gets out of Bed

As soon as Fred gets out of bed,
his underwear goes on his head.
His mother laughs, "Don't put it there,
a head's no place for underwear!"
But near his ears, above his brains,
is where Fred's underwear remains.

At night when Fred goes back to bed,
he deftly plucks it off his head.
His mother switches off the light
and softly croons, "Good night! Good night!"
And then, for reasons no one knows,
Fred's underwear goes on his toes.

Belinda Blue

Belinda Blue was furious,
she fumed, "I'm really mad!
This is the worst experience
that I have ever had."
She beat her fists against the wall,
she pounded on the floor,
"I am livid!" she exploded,
"I am bilious to the core!"

She wrung her hands, she tore her hair,
her tantrum grew and grew,
"I am angry, **angry, ANGRY!**"
shrieked enraged Belinda Blue.
She seemed to be beside herself,
she raced around the room,
she roared so loud, the neighbors thought
they'd heard a sonic boom.

Her rage was unabated,
it appeared she'd never quit,
in fact, she seemed to savor
every second of her fit,
Belinda Blue created
such an overwhelming scene
because at lunch, her mother said,
"Please eat just one green bean."

The Turkey Shot out of the Oven

The turkey shot out of the oven
and rocketed into the air,
it knocked every plate off the table
and partly demolished a chair.

It ricocheted into a corner
and burst with a deafening boom,
then splattered all over the kitchen,
completely obscuring the room.

It stuck to the walls and the windows,
it totally coated the floor,
there was turkey attached to the ceiling,
where there'd never been turkey before.

It blanketed every appliance,
it smeared every saucer and bowl,
there wasn't a way I could stop it,
that turkey was out of control.

I scraped and I scrubbed with displeasure,
and thought with chagrin as I mopped,
that I'd never again stuff a turkey
with popcorn that hadn't been popped.

I Am Wunk

I am Wunk, a wacky wizard,
and I wield a willow wand.
I wave it once, and there you swim,
a minnow in a pond.
I wave it twice, and there you sit,
a lizard on a log.
I wave it thrice, and there you fly,
a fly before a frog.

I am Wunk, a wily wizard,
and I hold a crystal sphere.
I spin it with my fingers,
you've a carrot in your ear.
I roll it on the table,
you've an anvil on your head.
I place it on your pillow,
you've a lion in your bed.

I am Wunk, a wondrous wizard,
and I wear a woolen hat.
I take it off and fold it,
you are smaller than a cat.
I put it in my pocket,
you are smaller than a mouse.
Do be quick, your doorbell's ringing . . .
I am Wunk outside your house.

Denson Dumm

Denson Dumm, with pomp and flair,
planted lightbulbs in his hair.
Now, however dark the night,
Denson Dumm is always bright.

You're Eating Like a Pig Again!

"You're eating like a pig again!"
my mother scolded me,
"If you keep eating like a pig,
a pig is what you'll be!"

I simply cannot fathom
what the fuss is all about,
and haven't I a lovely tail,
and see my splendid snout.

I Am Tired of Being Little

I am tired of being little,
I am sick of being thin,
I wish that I were giant size,
with whiskers on my chin.
No one would dare to tease me,
or to take away my toys,
for I would be much bigger
than the biggest bigger boys.

My folks would pay attention
to everything I said,
they couldn't make me eat my peas
or tell me, "Go to bed!"
I'd never be afraid again
if I were ten-foot-three,
I wish that I were giant size,
instead of small like me.

You're Nasty and You're Loud

You're nasty and you're loud,
you're mean enough for two.
If I could be a cloud,
I'd rain all day on you.

They Tell Me I'm Peculiar

They tell me I'm peculiar,
they seem to think I'm odd,
they look at me and grimace,
I smile at them and nod.

They cringe at my behavior,
"Unthinkable!" they say,
they're shocked that I love liver
and eat it every day.

I Should Have Stayed in Bed Today

I should have stayed in bed today,
in bed's where I belong,
as soon as I got up today,
things started going wrong,
I got a splinter in my foot,
my puppy made me fall,
I squirted toothpaste in my ear,
I crashed into the wall.

I knocked my homework off the desk,
it landed on my toes,
I spilled a glass of chocolate milk,
it's soaking through my clothes,
I accidentally bit my tongue,
that really made me moan,
and it was far from funny
when I banged my funny bone.

I scraped my knees, I bumped my nose,
I sat upon a pin,
I leapt up with alacrity,
and sharply barked my shin,
I stuck a finger in my eye,
the pain is quite severe,
I'd better get right back to bed
and stay there for a year.

Kevin the King of the Jungle

I'm Kevin the king of the jungle,
I live at the top of a tree,
although I behave like a monkey,
no lion is braver than me,
I swing through the air with abandon,
laughing a simian laugh,
I'm strong as my uncle gorilla,
I'm swift as my cousin giraffe.

I wrestle with dozens of gibbons,
I win, but they don't seem to mind,
I race with gazelles and impalas,
and frequently leave them behind,
hyenas and rhinos obey me,
great elephants do what I say,
and when I jump into the river,
fierce crocodiles hurry away.

I'm Kevin the king of the jungle,
I'm agile, I'm crafty, I'm bold,
green leaves are my only apparel,
and yet I have never caught cold,
my stepmother was a chimpanzee,
my stepfather was a baboon,
and that's why I eat with my fingers
instead of a fork or a spoon.

If I see a hippo look hungry,
I share a few edible roots,
when zebras or ostriches quarrel,
I settle their family disputes,
I'm Kevin the king of the jungle,
the lord of the leopard and gnu,
feel free to drop by my dominion,
I'll peel a banana for you.

Little Bird Outside My Window

Little bird outside my window,
I can hear you in my room
as you gaily serenade me
and eradicate the gloom.

Your chirping is the sweetest
that my ears have ever heard,
it awakens me each morning—
zip your beak up, little bird!

Unhappy South Pole Penguin

Unhappy South Pole penguin,
you are in a nasty mood
as you try to chew your dinner
which refuses to be chewed,
but a simple undertaking
will improve your attitude. . . .
you must first defrost your dinner,
for your dinner's frozen food.

Watson Watts

Watson Watts, atop his head,
balanced forty loaves of bread.
Forty loaves! no less, no more—
not one crumb fell to the floor.

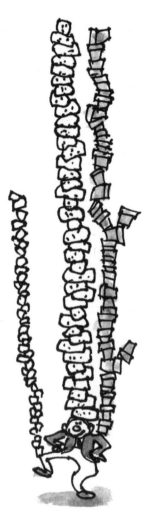

On his shoulders, Watson Watts
balanced forty flowerpots.
Forty pots! no more, no less—
yet he met with great success.

Watson balanced on his knees
forty chunks of Cheddar cheese.
Forty chunks! no less, no more—
just like loaves and pots before.

Watson Watts, upon his legs,
balanced forty ostrich eggs.
Forty eggs! no more, no less—
it took months to clean the mess!

Hello! How Are You? I Am Fine!

Hello! How are you? I am fine!
is all my dog will say,
he's probably repeated it
a thousand times today.
He doesn't bark his normal bark,
he doesn't even whine,
he only drones the same **Hello!**
How are you? I am fine!

Hello! How are you? I am fine!
his message doesn't change,
it's gotten quite monotonous,
and just a trifle strange.
Hello! How are you? I am fine!
it makes the neighbors stare,
they're unaware that yesterday
he ate my talking bear.

Life's Not Been the Same in My Family

Life's not been the same in my family
since the day that the new baby came,
my parents completely ignore me,
they scarcely remember my name.

The baby gets all their attention,
"Oh, isn't she precious!" they croon,
they think that she looks like an angel,
I think she resembles a prune.

They're thrilled when she giggles or gurgles,
"She burped!" they exclaim with delight,
they don't even mind when she wakes us
with deafening screams in the night.

They seem to believe she's a treasure,
there's simply no way I agree,
I wish she'd stop being a baby
and start being older than me.

I Met a Rat of Culture

I met a rat of culture
who was elegantly dressed
in a pair of velvet trousers
and a silver-buttoned vest,
he related ancient proverbs
and recited poetry,
he spoke a dozen languages,
eleven more than me.

That rat was perspicacious,
and had cogent things to say
on bionics, economics,
hydroponics, and ballet,
he instructed me in sculpture,
he shed light on keeping bees,
then he painted an acrylic
of an abstract view of cheese.

He had circled the equator,
he had visited the poles,
he extolled the art of sailing
while he baked assorted rolls,
he wove a woolen carpet
and he shaped a porcelain pot,
then he sang an operetta
while he danced a slow gavotte.

He was versed in jet propulsion,
an authority on trains,
all of botany and baseball
were contained within his brains,
he knew chemistry and physics,
he had taught himself to sew,
to my knowledge, there was nothing
that the rodent did not know.

He was vastly more accomplished
than the billions of his kin,
he performed a brief sonata
on a tiny violin,
but he squealed and promptly vanished
at the entrance of my cat,
for despite his erudition,
he was nothing but a rat.

Do Not Disturb the Woolly Wurbbe

Do not disturb the woolly Wurbbe
that scarcely seems to stir,
but sits upon the corner curb
and combs its curly fur.

There's nowhere that it cares to go,
it calmly stays in place
and grooms itself from head to toe,
contentment on its face.

To park upon that paving stone
is all it wants to do,
and if you leave the Wurbbe alone,
it will not bother you.

My Neighbor's Dog Is Purple

My neighbor's dog is purple,
its eyes are large and green,
its tail is almost endless,
the longest I have seen.

My neighbor's dog is quiet,
it does not bark one bit,
but when my neighbor's dog is near,
I feel afraid of it.

My neighbor's dog looks nasty,
it has a wicked smile. . . .
before my neighbor painted it,
it was a crocodile.

I Am a Ghost Who's Lost His Boo

I am a ghost who's lost his boo,
my boo is gone from me,
and I'm without a single clue
to where my boo might be.
It makes me mope, it makes me pout,
it almost makes me moan,
a ghost is not a ghost without
a boo to call his own.

My boo was piercing, fierce, and loud,
I used to strut and boast,
for I was positively proud
to be a gruesome ghost.
But now that I'm without a boo,
I find it rather weird,
there's little for a ghost to do
whose boo has disappeared.

Although I hover here and there,
and haunt a hundred rooms,
it seems there's no one I can scare
unless my boo resumes.
I am a ghost who's lost his boo,
alas! A boo I lack,
if you should find my boo, then you
had better give it back.

Last Night I Dreamed of Chickens

Last night I dreamed of chickens,
there were chickens everywhere,
they were standing on my stomach,
they were nesting in my hair,
they were pecking at my pillow,
they were hopping on my head,
they were ruffling up their feathers
as they raced about my bed.

They were on the chairs and tables,
they were on the chandeliers,
they were roosting in the corners,
they were clucking in my ears,
there were chickens, chickens, chickens
for as far as I could see. . . .
when I woke today, I noticed
there were eggs on top of me.

My Brother Built a Robot

My brother built a robot
that does not exactly work,
as soon as it was finished,
it began to go berserk,
its eyes grew incandescent
and its nose appeared to gleam,
it bellowed unbenignly
and its ears emitted steam.

My brother built that robot
to help us clean our room,
instead, it ate the dust pan
and attacked us with the broom,
it pulled apart our pillows,
it disheveled both our beds,
it took a box of crayons
and it doodled on our heads.

That robot seemed relentless
as it tied our socks in knots,
then clunked into the kitchen
and dismantled pans and pots,
the thing was not behaving
in the fashion we had planned,
it clanked into the bathroom
and it filled the tub with sand.

We tried to disconnect it,
but it was to no avail,
it picked us up and dropped us
in an empty garbage pail,
we cannot stop that robot,
for we're stymied by one hitch. . . .
my brother didn't bother
to equip it with a switch.

An Auk in Flight

An auk in flight
is sheer delight,
it soars above the sea.

An auk on land
is not so grand—
an auk walks **auk**wardly.

Fenton Phlantz

Fenton Phlantz is fairly weird,
he puts peanuts in his beard,
elephants are often found
following Fenton Phlantz around.

My Uncle Looked Me in the Eye

My uncle looked me in the eye
about an hour ago,
he said, "There are some things I think
that you had better know—
do not throw bricks at bumblebees
or grab a grizzly bear,
and never tug a tiger's tail
or pull a panther's hair.

"Don't wrestle with a rattlesnake
or ask a skunk to fight,
don't irritate an elephant
or tempt a lion to bite,
don't scuffle with a buffalo
or tease electric eels,
don't interrupt piranhas
at their underwater meals.

"Don't tickle a gorilla
   or invite a shark to smile,
   don't hug a hippopotamus
   or kiss a crocodile,
   don't ridicule a rhino
   or provoke a porcupine."
I've followed his advice so far,
   and I am doing fine.

Grasshopper Gumbo

GRASSHOPPER GUMBO

IGUANA TAIL TARTS

TOAD À LA MODE

PICKLED PELICAN PARTS

ELEPHANT GELATIN

FROG FRICASSEE

PURÉE OF PLATYPUS

BOILED BUMBLEBEE

PORCUPINE PUDDING

STEAMED CENTIPEDE SKINS

SQUID SUCKER SUNDAES

FRIED FLYING FISH FINS

MEADOW MOUSE MORSELS

CRACKED CROCODILE CRUNCH

The school cafeteria
serves them for lunch.

The Rains in Little Dribbles

The rains in Little Dribbles
are the sort one rarely sees,
every Thursday it pours cola,
Friday showers herbal teas,
early Saturday a sprinkle
of sweet cider fills the air,
then on Sunday sarsaparilla
soaks the citizenry there.

Monday morning, mocha malteds
softly saturate the town,
while on Tuesday lemon droplets
drizzle delicately down,
but the rain that rains on Wednesday
is a watermelon tide,
so the folks in Little Dribbles
spend their Wednesdays safe inside.

Today I Shall Powder My Elephant's Ears

Today I shall powder my elephant's ears
and paint his posterior red,
I'll trim all his toenails with suitable shears
and place a toupee on his head.

Tonight I shall tie a balloon to his tail
and wrap him in feathers and furs,
then fasten his necktie and velveteen veil
and put on his boots and his spurs.

There'll be a warm smile on my elephant's face
as we're welcomed to Pachyderm Hall,
to dance until daybreak with elegant grace
at the elephants' masquerade ball.

A Remarkable Adventure

I was at my bedroom table
with a notebook open wide,
when a giant anaconda
started winding up my side,
I was filled with apprehension
and retreated down the stairs,
to be greeted at the bottom
by a dozen grizzly bears.

We tumultuously tussled
till I managed to get free,
then I saw, with trepidation,
there were tigers after me,
I could feel them growing closer,
I was quivering with fear,
then I blundered into quicksand
and began to disappear.

I was rescued by an eagle
that descended from the skies
to embrace me with its talons,
to my terror and surprise,
but that raptor lost its purchase
when a blizzard made me sneeze,
and it dropped me in a thicket
where I battered both my knees.

I was suddenly surrounded
by a troop of savage trolls,
who maliciously informed me
they would toast me over coals,
I was lucky to elude them
when they briefly looked away—
that's the reason why my homework
isn't here with me today.

Squirrels

Squirrels, often found in parks,
have tails resembling question marks.
It's just coincidental, though. . . .
there's little squirrels care to know.

Katy Ate a Baked Potato

Katy ate a baked potato, strolling through the mews
in her yellow elevator alligator shoes.
That was Katy's last potato, she did not survive—
her elevator alligator shoes were still alive.

The Addle-pated Paddlepuss

The Addle-pated Paddlepuss
is agile as a cat,
its neck is long and limber,
and its face is broad and flat,
it moves with skill and vigor,
with velocity and grace,
as it spends its every second
playing Ping-Pong with its face.

The Addle-pated Paddlepuss
prevails in every game,
its opponent doesn't matter,
the result is all the same,
with its supersonic smashes
and its convoluted spins,
it demolishes all comers
and invariably wins.

The Addle-pated Paddlepuss,
with effervescent verve,
follows innovative volleys
with a scintillating serve,
if you're fond of playing Ping-Pong
and would like to lose in style,
the Addle-pated Paddlepuss
will serve you for awhile.

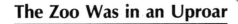

The Zoo Was in an Uproar

The zoo was in an uproar,
the rabbits stamped their feet,
the pigs expressed displeasure,
the gnus refused to eat,
"Disgraceful!" gabbed the gibbons,
"Barbaric!" boomed a bear,
"Distressing!" wept a leopard,
the ferrets fumed, *"Unfair!"*

"Repellant!" puled a puma,
"Bizarre!" a badger bawled,
  the donkeys were disgusted,
  the pandas were appalled,
  the camels ran for cover,
  a turtle fled her shell,
  the seals stayed underwater,
  a walrus felt unwell.

"How wicked!" whined a weasel,
"Uncalled for!" cawed the crows,
  the tigers lost their tempers,
  a polecat held his nose,
"Unseemly!" screamed the eagles,
  the lions roared with wrath,
  that day the hippopotamus
  forgot to take a bath.

Twaddletalk Tuck

I'm Twaddletalk Tuck and I talk and I talk
and I talk when I run and I talk when I walk
and I talk when I hop and I talk when I creep
and I talk when I wake and I talk when I sleep
and I talk when it's wet and I talk when it's dry
and I talk when I laugh and I talk when I cry
and I talk when I jump and I talk when I land
and I talk when I sit and I talk when I stand
and I talk and I talk into anyone's ear
and I talk and I talk when there's nobody near
and I talk when I'm hoarse and my voice is a squawk
for I'm Twaddletalk Tuck and I talk and I talk.

Slow Sloth's Slow Song

I . . . . *am* . . . . *a* . . . . *sloth* . . . .
a . . . . *sloth* . . . . *am* . . . . *I* . . . .
I . . . . *live* . . . . *in* . . . . *trees* . . . .
But . . . . *I* . . . . *can't* . . . . *fly* . . . .
I . . . . *do* . . . . *not* . . . . *run* . . . .
I . . . . *am* . . . . *so* . . . . *slow* . . . .
But . . . . *I* . . . . *am* . . . . *where* . . . .
I . . . . *want* . . . . *to* . . . . *go* .

My Mother Made a Meat Loaf

My mother made a meat loaf
that provided much distress,
she tried her best to serve it,
but she met with no success,
her sharpest knife was powerless
to cut a single slice,
and her efforts with a cleaver
failed completely to suffice.

She whacked it with a hammer,
and she smacked it with a brick,
but she couldn't faze that meat loaf,
it remained without a nick,
I decided I would help her
and assailed it with a drill,
but the drill made no impression,
though I worked with all my skill.

We chipped at it with chisels,
but we didn't make a dent,
it appeared my mother's meat loaf
was much harder than cement,
then we set upon that meat loaf
with a hatchet and an ax,
but that meat loaf stayed unblemished
and withstood our fierce attacks.

We borrowed bows and arrows,
and we fired at close range,
it didn't make a difference,
for that meat loaf didn't change,
we beset it with a blowtorch,
but we couldn't find a flaw,
and we both were flabbergasted
when it broke the power saw.

We hired a hippopotamus
to trample it around,
but that meat loaf was so mighty
that it simply stood its ground,
now we manufacture meat loaves
by the millions, all year long,
they are famous in construction,
building houses tall and strong.

We're Know-nothing Neebies

We're Know-nothing Neebies
with nothing to say,
and certain to say it
without a delay,
we're perfectly pompous,
indelibly dense,
we haven't a trace
of a semblance of sense.

We're Know-nothing Neebies,
complacent and proud,
the things we don't know
we proclaim very loud,
from summer to winter,
from spring until fall,
we daily display
we know nothing at all.

We're Know-nothing Neebies,
invincibly vain,
distinguished by pates
with no space for a brain,
you cannot avoid us,
we've never been rare,
just look all around you,
we're found everywhere.

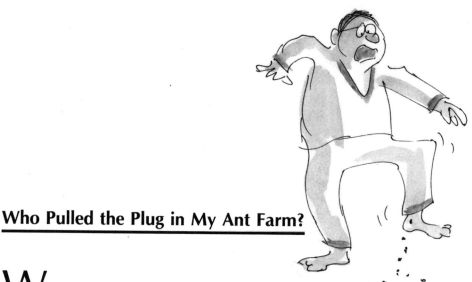

Who Pulled the Plug in My Ant Farm?

Who pulled the plug in my ant farm?
Who let my ants get away?
Their tunnels are almost deserted,
I'm having a miserable day.
They've gathered in groups in the corners,
they're swarming all over the floor,
for each one I get in my clutches,
there seem to be two dozen more.

I'm doing my best to corral them,
I doubt that I'll ever be done,
there's nothing as hard to recapture
as hundreds of ants on the run.
My mother found ants in her slippers,
my sister found ants in her shoes,
they got in my father's pajamas,
he bellowed, "I'm blowing a fuse!"

Some have invaded the kitchen,
they've started attacking our food,
my mother is shrieking in horror,
and I'm in a horrible mood.
Who pulled the plug in my ant farm,
infesting our home with those pests?
I have the unhappy suspicion
that ants are our permanent guests.

Today I'm Going Yesterday

Today I'm going yesterday
as quickly as I can,
I'm confident I'll do it,
I've devised a clever plan,
it involves my running backward
at a constant rate of speed,
if I'm mindful of my timing,
I'll undoubtedly succeed.

Today I'm going yesterday,
I'm moving very fast
as I'm putting off the future
for the rather recent past,
I can feel the present fading
as I hastily depart,
and look forward to arriving
on the day before I start.

Today I'm going yesterday,
I'm slipping out of sight
and anticipate I'll vanish
just a bit before tonight,
when I reach my destination,
I'll compose a note to say
that I'll see you all tomorrow,
which of course will be today.

There's No One as Slow as Slomona

There's no one as slow as Slomona,
Slomona's unbearably slow,
it takes her as long to eat breakfast
as it takes a tomato to grow,
she sits in the kitchen all morning
and nibbles a morsel of bread,
she dawdles so long at the table,
it's time to get ready for bed.

There's no one as slow as Slomona,
her pace makes molasses seem fast,
she once raced a snail and a turtle
and finished a definite last,
she never does anything quickly,
but inches along at a crawl,
one winter she sat on a splinter
and didn't shout "Ouch!" until fall.

Don't Yell at Me!

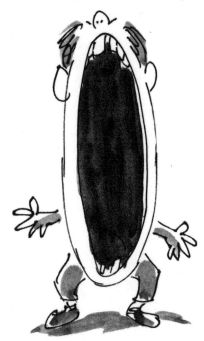

Don't yell at me!
Don't yell at me!
I hate it when you do,
it makes me feel so miserable,
I want to run from you.
I simply cannot stand it
when you scream into my ear,
if I knew how to do it,
I'd completely disappear.

Don't yell at me!
Don't yell at me!
I'll crawl away and hide,
I'll detonate to smithereens
or shrivel up inside.
Feel free to thumb your nose at me,
or wiggle all your toes at me,
or even ring a bell at me,
but please, **please, please,**
DON'T YELL AT ME!

Nigel Gline

When Nigel Gline sat down to dine,
he yawned, "This meal's a bore!
It's nothing more than what I've had
a thousand times before.
I'm through with cheese and chocolate,
I'm done with beans and beef,
I'd like a tasty tree instead."
So Nigel ate a leaf.

He liked that leaf, and swallowed more,
then nibbled on a twig,
that hardly seemed to be enough,
his appetite was big,
the twigs were so delicious
that he started on a limb,
soon every branch upon that tree
had vanished into him.

"It's time to try the trunk!" he said,
and ate it on the spot,
the bark was easy to digest,
the knots, of course, were not.
Now Nigel Gline declines to dine,
deep roots grow from his toes,
and birds nest in the leafy boughs
that stem from Nigel's nose.

They Never Send Sam to the Store Anymore

The day they sent Sam to the grocery store
to purchase a carton of eggs,
he brought back a pear with a pearl in its core,
and a leopard with lavender legs.

He returned with an elephant small as a mouse,
a baseball that bounces a mile,
a little tame dragon that heats up the house,
and a lantern that lights when they smile.

Sam brought them a snowball that never feels cold,
a gossamer carpet that flies,
a salmon of silver, a grackle of gold,
and an ermine with emerald eyes.

They never send Sam to the store anymore,
no matter how often he begs,
for he brought back a dodo that danced on the floor,
but he didn't bring home any eggs.

I Wave Good-bye When Butter Flies

I wave good-bye when butter flies
and cheer a boxing match,
I've often watched my pillow fight,
I've sewn a cabbage patch,
I like to dance at basket balls
or lead a rubber band,
I've marvelled at a spelling bee,
I've helped a peanut stand.

It's possible a pencil points,
but does a lemon drop?
Does coffee break or chocolate kiss,
and will a soda pop?
I share my milk with drinking straws,
my meals with chewing gum,
and should I see my pocket change,
I'll hear my kettle drum.

It makes me sad when lettuce leaves,
I laugh when dinner rolls,
I wonder if the kitchen sinks
and if a salad bowls,
I've listened to a diamond ring,
I've waved a football fan,
and if a chimney sweeps the floor,
I'm sure the garbage can.

My Frog Is a Frog

My frog is a frog that is hopelessly hoarse,
my frog is a frog with a reason, of course,
my frog is a frog that cannot croak a note,
my frog is a frog with a frog in its throat.

Wilhelmina Wafflewitz

I'm Wilhelmina Wafflewitz,
I never can decide
the things I think I'd like to do,
although I think I've tried.
What should I wear? When should I eat?
Where do I want to go?
Should I do this, or that instead?
I never seem to know.

I'm Wilhelmina Wafflewitz,
and I'm afraid I find
it practically impossible
to know what's on my mind.
Since I'm unsure of what to do,
I think I'll stay quite still,
at least, I think, I think I think,
I think I think I will.

I'm Off to Catch a Bumblebee

I'm off to catch a bumblebee,
so bumblebees beware!
I've brought the best equipment,
with accessories to spare—
a bottle full of buttons
and a carton full of corks,
assorted socks and saucers
and a gross of broken forks.

I'm off to catch a bumblebee,
I'll surely find one soon,
I've got a pound of pepper
and a helium balloon,
my trusty feather duster
and eleven bars of soap,
a pair of pop-up toasters
and a leaky periscope.

I have brought my beach umbrella,
I have brought my Hula Hoop,
my yo-yo and viola
and a bowl of chicken soup,
a lariat that's large enough
to loop about a bear—
I'm off to catch a bumblebee,
so bumblebees beware!

I Am Digging a Hole in the Ceiling

I am digging a hole in the ceiling
in order to gaze at the sky,
I began at the end of September,
I intend to be done by July.

I suppose I might look out the windows,
but they aren't sufficiently clean,
and it's far too much trouble to wash them,
for I haven't the proper machine.

I could leave by the door if I chose to,
I am sure I'd succeed if I tried,
but the handle's been stuck since November,
and the weather is nasty outside.

So I'm digging a hole in the ceiling
to study the sun and the moon,
I suspect it will take until summer,
for I'm using a very small spoon.

The Spider

The spider, sly and talented,
weaves silver webs of silken thread,
then waits for unobservant flies
. . . to whom she'll not apologize!

Bats

Bats have shiny leather wings,
bats do many clever things,
bats doze upside-down by day,
bats come out at night to play.

Bats cavort in soaring cliques,
sounding ultrasonic shrieks,
acrobatic in the sky,
bats catch every bug they spy.

Captain Conniption

I'm Captain Conniption,
the scourge of the sea,
no pirate alive
is as fearsome as me,
I'm ten times as tough
as the skin of a whale,
the sharks cringe in terror
wherever I sail.

I'm Captain Conniption,
the bane of the fleet,
I don't wash my face,
and I don't wash my feet,
I wear a black hat
and I fly a black flag,
I'm bad as can be,
though I don't like to brag.

When I'm on the deck
with my cutlass in hand,
the saltiest sailors
start sailing for land,
they know I'm the nastiest
nautical knave,
and bold as a brigand
is bound to behave.

I'm Captain Conniption,
and up to no good,
you'll soon walk the plank
if I think that you should,
I'd show you right now
how I vanquish a foe,
but I hear my mother,
so I have to go.

My Younger Brother's Appetite

My younger brother's appetite
is finicky, and very slight,
he's almost guaranteed to hate
whatever's placed upon his plate.
"I will not eat these greens!" he groans,
"This chicken has too many bones,
the cantaloupe is far too sweet,
there's too much gravy on the meat."

He whines, "The salad tastes like soap,
the macaroni's more like rope,
I cannot stand these soggy peas,
and I won't touch this awful cheese!"
My younger brother doesn't eat
enough to fill a parakeet.
However did he get to be
the size and shape of two of me?

I'm Sorry!

I'm sorry I squashed a banana in bed,
I'm sorry I bandaged a whole loaf of bread,
I'm sorry I pasted the prunes to your pants,
I'm sorry I brought home the ants.

I'm sorry for letting the dog eat the broom,
I'm sorry for freeing a frog in your room,
I'm sorry I wrote on the wall with sardines,
I'm sorry I sat on the beans.

I'm sorry for putting the peas in my hair,
I'm sorry for leaving the eggs on your chair,
I'm sorry for tying a can to the cat,
I'm sorry for being a brat!

We Moved About a Week Ago

We moved about a week ago,
it's nice here, I suppose,
the trouble is, I miss my friends,
like Beth, who bopped my nose,
and Jess, who liked to wrestle
and dump me in the dirt,
and Liz, who found a garter snake
and put it down my shirt.

I miss my friend Fernando,
he sometimes pulled my hair,
I miss his sister Sarah,
she shaved my teddy bear,
I miss the Trumble triplets
who dyed my sneakers blue,
and Gus, who broke my glider,
I guess I miss him too.

I really miss Melissa
who chased me up a tree,
I even miss "Gorilla" Brown
who used to sit on me,
the more I think about them,
the more it makes me sad,
I hope I make some friends here
as great as those I had.

Four Vain and Ancient Tortoises

Four vain and ancient tortoises
upon a balmy shore
were aimlessly debating
who was slowest of the four.
"I'm slowest here!" said tortoise one,
said tortoise two, "I crawl!"
"I'm sure it's me!" said tortoise three,
said four, "I'm worst of all!"

"We'll hold a race!" said tortoise one,
said tortoise two, "Agreed!"
said three and four, "We'll thus compare
our utter lack of speed!"
"I'll lose, of course!" said tortoise one,
said two, "I'll not prevail!"
said three, "I'll wind up far behind!"
said tortoise four, "I'll fail!"

Four vain and ancient tortoises
began their foolish race,
and since they were all tortoises,
they set a sluggish pace.
"I'm trailing now!" said tortoise one,
said tortoise two, "I'm last!"
"I disagree!" said tortoise three,
said four, "You're all too fast!"

Then neck and neck and neck and neck,
the finish line was crossed,
and none of them had won the race,
and none of them had lost.
"You've bested me!" said tortoise one,
said two, "My loss is sweet!"
said three, "I've shown I'm last alone!"
said four, "I've met defeat!"

And so they go on boasting
of how slowly they had run,
each futilely insisting
that the other three had won.
They argue indecisively,
no wiser than before,
four vain and ancient tortoises
upon a balmy shore.

A Goat Wandered into a Junkyard

A goat wandered into a junkyard
in search of an afternoon meal,
he started with remnants of rubber
and several fragments of steel.
He nibbled a couple of axles,
he gobbled up gauges and gears,
he gnawed on a tangle of wires
and colorful plastic veneers.

He polished off various bearings,
he munched on a mountain of brass,
he bolted a heap of upholstery
and numerous panels of glass.
He put away pistons and pedals,
then followed a fender or two
with most of a standard transmission,
and they aren't easy to chew.

He ate an assortment of sprockets,
he swallowed some springs by the coil,
then washed down his lunch with a gallon
of forty-weight premium oil.
As soon as that goat had digested
his odd but industrious meal,
he coughed and he coughed and he coughed
    and he coughed
and he coughed up an automobile.

The Disputatious Deeble

I'm the Disputatious Deeble,
who is bound to disagree
with anything at any time
you ever say to me.
"It's freezing!" you may shiver,
I'll reply, "It's far too hot!"
and if you claim, "It's raining!"
I'll rebuff you, "No! It's not!"

I'm the Disputatious Deeble,
contradictory all the time,
if you remark, "A lemon!"
I'll annunciate, "A lime!"
"Sweet butter!" you may comment,
I'll correct you, "Salty cheese!"
and if you call out, "Carrots!"
I will persevere with "Peas!"

I'm the Disputatious Deeble,
disharmonious and cross,
if you say, "Lovely gravy!"
I'll insist, "An awful sauce!"
Should you proclaim, "It's sunny!"
I'll retort, "A cloudy night!"
and I am never never wrong,
and you are never right.

I Wish My Father Wouldn't Try to Fix Things Anymore

My father's listed everything
he's planning to repair,
I hope he won't attempt it,
for the talent isn't there,
he tinkered with the toaster
when the toaster wouldn't pop,
now we keep it disconnected,
but we cannot make it stop.

He fiddled with the blender,
and he took a clock apart,
the clock is running backward,
and the blender will not start,
every windowpane he's puttied
now admits the slightest breeze,
and he's half destroyed the furnace,
if we're lucky, we won't freeze.

102

The TV set was working,
yet he thought he'd poke around,
now the picture's out of focus,
and there isn't any sound,
there's a faucet in the basement
that had dripped one drop all year,
since he fixed it, we can't find it
without wearing scuba gear.

I wish my father wouldn't try
to fix things anymore,
for everything he's mended
is more broken than before,
if my father finally fixes
every item on his list,
we'll be living in the garden,
for our house will not exist.

Benita Beane

Benita Beane, the trumpet queen,
makes audiences cheer,
she does not play the normal way,
she only plays by ear.

The Fuddies

The Fuddies fly above the dale,
and as they bumble by,
they leave a long and muddy trail
of footprints in the sky.

There's a Worm in My Apple

There's a worm in my apple,
a bug in my pear,
a beetle has managed
to get in my hair,
I swatted the gnat
that was nipping my ear,
and a hornet is buzzing
uncomfortably near.

The ants in the kitchen
are stealing the bread,
while a mouse sets up housekeeping
under my bed,
wherever I look
I encounter a moth,
and a fly just decided
to dive in the broth.

There's a spider outside
that would like to move in,
a pair of mosquitoes
are riddling my chin,
the rat in the attic's
determined to stay,
I'm facing a fairly
pestiferous day.

Try Never to Tickle the Twickles

Try never to tickle the Twickles,
 the Twickles, when tickled, may smile,
"We do not like smiling!" they snivel,
"It's vulgar! It's vapid! It's vile!"
 If ever you tickle the Twickles,
 the Twickles are likely to grin,
"Unthinkable!" whimper the Twickles,
"It ruins the shape of the chin!"

 I repeat, never tickle the Twickles,
 the Twickles may laugh if you do,
"It goes against nature!" they grumble,
"It's clearly considered taboo!"
 Still worse, if you tickle the Twickles,
 the Twickles are apt to guffaw,
"Guffawing's disgraceful!" they clamor,
"We recently made it a law!"

108

The Twickles you tickle will chuckle,
the Twickles you tickle will roar,
"Deplorable!" blubber the Twickles,
"It's not what we Twickles are for!
Untickled, we Twickles are grateful,
we Twickles untickled are glad,
ignore our morose dispositions,
we're happiest when we are sad!"

Warteena Weere Just Bit My Ear

Warteena Weere just bit my ear,
she mopped my face with dirt,
she popped a glop of bubblegum
and dropped it down my shirt.

She plopped her ice cream in my hair,
she bopped me with her shoe,
I think Warteena likes me—
I think I like her too!

Fuzzy, You Are Underfoot!

Fuzzy, you are underfoot!
You're never still, you won't stay put,
you twirl and try to catch your tail,
and never notice that you fail.
You clamber up and down the stairs,
depositing unsightly hairs,
and when it's time to go outside,
you scamper off and try to hide.

Fuzzy, though you understand,
you never follow my command,
I tell you "Sit!" I tell you "Stay!"
You lick my face and run away.
I buy you bones, and yet you choose
to gnaw the chair, to chew my shoes,
I would not mind a dog like that,
but you're peculiar for a cat.

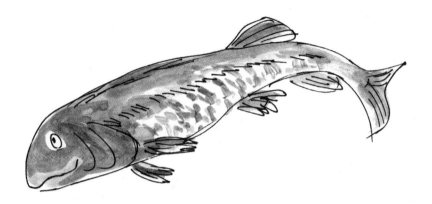

I Am Sitting Here and Fishing

I am sitting here and fishing
with my trusty rod and reel,
though I'd like to catch a snapper,
I would not refuse an eel,
and a pike would be delightful,
and a cod would be okay,
and a bass would be fantastic,
and a dace would make my day.

I am hoping for a haddock,
I am eager for a bream,
and a perch would be perfection,
and a pompano supreme,
I'd be grateful for a grunion,
I would find a flounder fine,
I'd be tickled with a pickerel
or a mackerel on my line.

But I've yet to get a nibble
at this little fishing hole,
I've not seen a single salmon
or a solitary sole,
not a miniature minnow,
not the sorriest sardine . . .
when you're fishing in the desert,
fish are few and far between.

My Woolen Sweater Itches Me

My woolen sweater itches me,
I scratch until I squeal.
Of course, I'm free to take it off . . .
just think how sheep must feel!

I'm Much Too Tired to Play Tonight

I'm much too tired to play tonight,
I'm much too tired to talk,
I'm much too tired to pet the dog
or take him for a walk,
I'm much too tired to bounce a ball,
I'm much too tired to sing,
I'm much too tired to try to think
about a single thing.

I'm much too tired to laugh tonight,
I'm much too tired to smile,
I'm much too tired to watch TV
or read a little while,
I'm much too tired to drink my milk
or even nod my head,
but I'm not nearly tired enough
to have to go to bed.

My Snake

My snake, a long and limber pet,

is practicing the alphabet,

he demonstrates immense finesse

in shaping a curvaceous S .

He follows his initial show

by closing up into an O ,

then fabricates an F and G

with enviable artistry.

My snake, with neither pad nor pen,

delineates a splendid N ,

an agile H , a supple L ,

an X with little parallel,

a shapely J , a graceful A ,

a seamless C , a clever K ,

then pausing for a breath or two,

he turns himself into a U .

My snake, with every skillful twist,

appends a letter to his list,

he makes an E , he forms an M ,

a Y and V come after them,

he diagrams a dextrous D ,

a subtle T , a nimble Z ,

a convoluted curly Q ,

a virtuoso W .

My snake, performing like a star,

portrays a P , enacts an R ,

contorts into a brilliant B

with stylish sinuosity.

And yet, though he may stretch and shake,

one single point eludes my snake,

despite his most ingenious try,

he simply cannot dot his I .

My Brother Is a Quarterback

My brother is a quarterback,
I rarely catch a pass,
and he can run a marathon,
I soon run out of gas,
he pitches for his baseball team,
I pop up on his curve,
and he's an ace at tennis,
I can't return his serve.

My brother dunks the basketball,
I dribble like a mule,
he swims like a torpedo,
I flounder in the pool,
he's accurate at archery,
I hardly ever score,
he boxes and he wrestles,
I wind up on the floor.

My brother catches lots of fish,
I haven't any luck,
he's captain of his hockey team,
I can't control the puck,
his bowling's unbelievable,
I bowl like a buffoon,
he says someday I'll start to win . . .
I hope someday is soon.

I Want a Pet Porcupine, Mother

"I want a pet porcupine, Mother!"
I said to her early today,
she chuckled, "It's out of the question,
I wish you would go out and play."

"Then, Mother, I want a gorilla,
or else I would like a giraffe!"
she answered without hesitation,
"Ridiculous! Don't make me laugh!"

"Then, Mother, I want an iguana,
 a burro, a boar, or a bear!"
 she seemed to start growing impatient,
 she shouted, "Get out of my hair!"

"Then, Mother, I want a pet lion,
 I'm certain a lion would do,
 I'd take him for walks every Sunday
 to visit his friends in the zoo!"

"You can't have a lion!" she told me,
 "Be glad with the pet that you've got!"
 I guess we're just keeping the rhino,
 she's always liked Rhona a lot.

Mold, Mold

Mold, mold,
marvelous mold,
alluring to look at,
enthralling to hold,
you are so delightful
I can't help but smile
when I nuzzle a smidgen
of mold for awhile.

Slime, slime,
savory slime,
you're luscious and succulent
any old time,
there's hardly a thing
that is nearly as grand
as a dollop of slime
in the palm of my hand.

Some think you are miserable
manners of muck,
they can't stand to see you,
you make them say, "Yuck!"
But I think you're fetching,
beguiling and fine,
mold, you are glorious,
slime, you're divine.

My Family's Sleeping Late Today

My family's sleeping late today,
but I am wide awake,
and making all the racket
it is possible to make.
I'm rapping on a window pane,
I'm hammering a nail,
I'm playing tackle with the cat,
and yanking on her tail.

I'm racing madly through the house,
I'm slamming every door,
I'm imitating jungle sounds,
I trumpet and I roar.
I think I'll play my tambourine
and pop a big balloon,
they'll never sleep through all of that,
they're sure to get up soon.

I Did Not Eat Your Ice Cream

I did not eat your ice cream,
I did not swipe your socks,
I did not stuff your lunch box
with rubber bands and rocks.

I did not hide your sweater,
I did not dent your bike,
it must have been my sister,
we look a lot alike.

Sir Bottomwide

Sir Bottomwide, a stalwart knight,
was absolutely blue,
he sniveled inconsolably,
he sobbed the whole day through,
he blubbered as he clanked about,
he cried astride his horse,
the teardrops flooded from his eyes
with unabated force.

They fell upon his pillow
while he slumbered in his bed,
they leaked into his regal ears,
they drenched his noble head.
Sir Bottomwide had cause to be
a most unhappy knight,
his cast-iron armored underwear
was half a size too tight.

The Moodles Have No Middles

The Moodles have no middles,
though they're otherwise complete,
their faces are bass fiddles,
which they play upon the street.
It's apparent, if you've seen them
in their bands of tens and twelves,
that there's nothing in-between them
to connect them to themselves.

The Moodles love to chatter,
and the Moodles love to sport,
despite a lack of matter
to provide them with support.
It's a mystifying riddle
that's impossible to guess,
how those Moodles with no middles
can survive with such success.

The Barber of Shrubbery Hollow

I'm the barber of Shrubbery Hollow,
I need neither clippers nor comb,
I never trim anyone's whiskers,
nor manicure anyone's dome.
My services aren't required,
no customers come to my shop
requesting a shave and a haircut,
not even "a bit off the top!"

I'm the barber of Shrubbery Hollow,
with practically nothing to do,
I spend the day sharpening scissors
or giving my shoes a shampoo.
I might as well go out of business
and give up this boring routine,
for why bother being a barber
where everyone's bald as a bean?

Picklepuss Pearl

I'm Picklepuss Pearl, and I'm not very nice,
I'm not made of sugar, I'm not made of spice,
my attitude's awful, my temper is vile,
I have no idea what it feels like to smile.

I'm Picklepuss Pearl, and I'm nasty and sour,
my wretched expression can wither a flower,
it takes but a blink of my miserable eye
for laughing hyenas to break down and cry.

If I fix your face with my permanent frown,
your stomach is liable to turn upside-down,
my stare is so cold it turns water to ice,
I'm Picklepuss Pearl, and I'm not very nice.

My Brother Is as Generous as Anyone Could Be

My brother is as generous
as anyone could be,
for everything he's ever had
he's always shared with me.
He has loaned me his binoculars,
his new computer games,
and his wind-up walking dragon
that breathes artificial flames.

I've been grateful for his robots,
for his giant teddy bear,
but not for certain other things
I'd hoped he'd never share—
Though I'm glad he's shared his rockets
and his magic jumping rocks,
I wish my brother hadn't shared
his case of chicken pox.

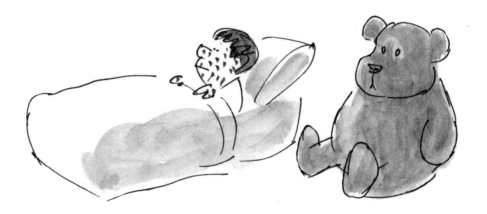

I Lost My Invisible Puppy

I lost my invisible puppy
when we were out walking today,
she disappeared into the bushes
and totally faded away.

My puppy is not too apparent,
my puppy is paler than pale,
she tends not to draw much attention,
she wags an invisible tail.

She wears an invisible collar,
her leash is invisible too,
I fear that she's vanished forever,
she's totally hidden from view.

I'll miss her obscure little antics,
her odd indiscernible tricks,
she chased inconspicuous crickets,
she fetched undetectable sticks.

My poor imperceptible puppy
is probably still in the park,
perhaps if I pay close attention,
I'll hear her inaudible bark.

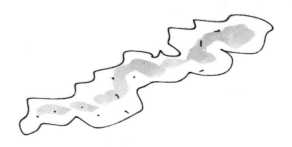

The Smoking Yokadokas

We're the Smoking Yokadokas,
we sincerely need to smoke,
and we do not mind the slightest
that our smoking makes you choke,
our malodorous miasma
will assail you when we're near,
it will irritate your nostrils
and compel your eyes to tear.

We're the Smoking Yokadokas,
we're not nice to have around,
you can often hear us coughing,
it's a coarse and raucous sound,
all our teeth are brown and yellow,
and our breath is always stale,
we're especially offensive
at the moment we exhale.

Our appearance is unsightly,
we have ashes on our clothes,
our aroma is appalling,
you may have to hold your nose,
but don't waste your time complaining
we contaminate the air,
we're the Smoking Yokadokas,
and we simply do not care.

Mosquitoes, Mosquitoes!

Mosquitoes, mosquitoes,
stop torturing me,
why can't you behave
more considerately,
you've bitten me practically
down to the bone,
mosquitoes, mosquitoes,
please leave me alone!

Mosquitoes, mosquitoes,
you're hard to ignore,
I itch and I scratch,
I can't stand anymore,
you've bitten my bottom,
you've bitten my top,
mosquitoes, mosquitoes,
I'm begging you, stop!

Mosquitoes, mosquitoes,
I honestly feel
it's time that you went
somewhere else for a meal,
you've bitten me places
I can't even see,
mosquitoes, mosquitoes,
stop torturing me!

I Saw a Brontosaurus

I saw a brontosaurus
saunter through my neighborhood,
this struck me as peculiar,
as I'd heard they'd gone for good,
its proportions were imposing,
it was long and tall and wide,
I ran home to fetch a ladder,
then ascended for a ride.

It was hard to sit astride it,
for its hide was rather rough
and I had to ride it bareback,
there's no saddle big enough,
it turned into the sunset
and we started heading west,
my parents seemed uneasy,
but the neighbors looked impressed.

We squeezed between the buildings
as we thundered out of town,
the beast became rambunctious,
and it bounded up and down,
it ignored my agitation
and my frequent shouts of "Whoa!"
and I almost bounced to pieces
as we crossed a wide plateau.

That brontosaurus tossed me
in the middle of a plain,
I landed in a wheat field,
where I fell against the grain,
though I treasure my adventure,
I won't do it anymore,
for that bucking brontosaurus
made my bottom bronto**sore!**

Rhododendra Rosenbloom

Rhododendra Rosenbloom
loves the smell of fine perfume,
she went to the corner store,
there she bought perfumes galore—

BUTTERCUP BANANA PEEL

CATERPILLAR CAMOMILE

ROSE REPUGNANT RAT REGRET

VINYL VIPER VIOLET

GREEN FARINA WILLOW THRILL

DROMEDARY DAFFODIL

FRANGIAPANI FINGERNAIL

GLADIOLA GARBAGE PAIL

SLOPPY GUPPY POPPY PINE

TULIP TURTLE TURPENTINE

Rhododendra Rosenbloom
bought ten kinds of fine perfume,
she could not have purchased more—
it was just a ten scent store!

I'm Certain I Sing Like an Angel

I'm certain I sing like an angel,
I have a mellifluous voice,
the moment I open my musical mouth,
the multitudes ought to rejoice.

I croon with melodic precision
in tones undeniably sweet,
I wonder why people throw water at me
whenever I sing in the street.

Why Do I Water My Flowers?

Why do I water my flowers?
Why do I turn on the hose
to bathe my beloved begonias
and spray every beautiful rose?
Why do I tend to my tulips
and cover them lightly with dew?
Why do I sprinkle my lilacs?
I haven't come up with a clue.

Why do I drench my azaleas,
carnations, and sweet columbine?
Why do I dampen the blossoms
that grace my wisteria vine?
It's foolish to water my flowers,
I really don't know why I try—
They're all manufactured of plastic,
and manage just fine when they're dry.

Super Samson Simpson

I am Super Samson Simpson,
I'm superlatively strong,
I like to carry elephants,
I do it all day long,
I pick up half a dozen
and hoist them in the air,
it's really somewhat simple,
for I have strength to spare.

My muscles are enormous,
they bulge from top to toe,
and when I carry elephants,
they ripple to and fro,
but I am not the strongest
in the Simpson family,
for when I carry elephants,
my grandma carries me.

As Soon as Penny Goes to Bed

As soon as Penny goes to bed,
she screeches and she cries,
she tosses on her pillow
and she cannot shut her eyes.

She whimpers and she snivels
and she blubbers and she wails. . . .
poor Penny should not try to sleep
upon a bed of nails.

The Wumpaloons, Which Never Were

The Wumpaloons, which never were,
had silver scales and purple fur,
their wings were alabaster white,
their manes as black as anthracite,
their legs were pink and indigo,
with toes of bright pistachio,
their noses were a bottle green,
their antlers tan and tangerine.

The Wumpaloons had crimson lips,
their tails were teal, with flaxen tips,
their lilac eyes were flecked with dots
as gold as summer apricots,
their necks were lemon, striped with blue,
their ears were of a ruby hue.
How nice to think they might occur,
the Wumpaloons, which never were.

My Fish Can Ride a Bicycle

My fish can ride a bicycle,
my fish can climb a tree,
my fish enjoys a glass of milk,
my fish takes naps with me.

My fish can play the clarinet,
my fish can bounce a ball,
my fish is not like other fish,
my fish can't swim at all.

My Sister Ate an Orange

My sister ate an orange,
I'm astonished that she did,
she swallowed it completely,
she's a disconcerting kid.

My sister ate an orange,
first she chewed it for awhile,
then digested it entirely
with a silly sort of smile.

My sister ate an orange,
it's a novel thing to do,
then she also ate a yellow
and a purple and a blue.

An Elephant Is Hard to Hide

An elephant is hard to hide,
it's rather tall, it's fairly wide,
it occupies a lot of space,
you just can't put it anyplace.
It's quite an unrewarding chore
to try and cram it in a drawer,
a closet's somewhat better, but
you're apt to find the door won't shut.

An elephant beneath your bed
will manifest both tail and head,
and in the tub, there's little doubt
that it will soon be singled out.
An elephant won't simply sit,
it tends to move about a bit,
this trait, when coupled with its size
makes it a nightmare to disguise.

An elephant, if kept around
is almost certain to be found,
your parents may suspect one's near
when peanuts start to disappear.
An elephant is hard to hide,
I know it's so, because I've tried,
my family should detect mine soon . . .
I brought it home this afternoon.

Mother Goblin's Lullaby

Go to sleep, my baby goblin,
hushaby, my dear of dears,
if you disobey your mother,
she will twist your pointed ears.

Little goblin, stop complaining,
time for all your eyes to close,
if you make your mother angry,
she will bite your tiny nose.

Slumber sweetly till tomorrow,
do not worry, Mother's near,
dream of demons weirdly screaming,
hushaby, my goblin dear.

My Brother's Bug

My brother's bug was green and plump,
it did not run, it could not jump,
it had no fur for it to shed,
it slept all night beneath his bed.

My brother's bug had dainty feet,
it did not need a lot to eat,
it did not need a lot to drink,
it did not scream, it did not stink.

It always tried to be polite,
it did not scratch, it did not bite,
the only time it soiled the rug
was when I squashed my brother's bug.

We're Fearless Flying Hotdogs

We're fearless flying hotdogs,
the famous "Unflappable Five,"
we're mustered in formation
to climb, to dip, to dive,
we spread our wings with relish,
then reach for altitude,
we're aerobatic wieners,
the fastest flying food.

We're fearless flying hotdogs,
we race with flair and style,
then catch up with each other
and soar in single file,
you never saw such daring,
such power and control,
as when we swoop and spiral,
then slide into a roll.

The throngs applaud our antics,
they cheer us long and loud,
there's never a chilly reception,
there's never a sour crowd,
and if we may speak frankly,
we are a thrilling sight,
we're fearless flying hotdogs,
the delicate essence of flight.

Index to Titles

Addle-pated Paddlepuss, The, 60
As Soon As Fred Gets Out of Bed, 14
As Soon as Penny Goes to Bed, 144
Auk in Flight, An, 48

Barber of Shrubbery Hollow, The, 128
Bats, 89
Belinda Blue, 16
Benita Beane, 104

Captain Conniption, 90

Denson Dumm, 22
Disputatious Deeble, The, 100
Do Not Disturb the Woolly Wurbbe, 40
Don't Yell at Me!, 75

Early Worm Got Out of Bed, An, 8
Elephant Is Hard to Hide, An, 148

Fenton Phlantz, 49
Four Vain and Ancient Tortoises, 96
Fuddies, The, 105
Fuzzy, You Are Underfoot!, 111

Goat Wandered into a Junkyard, A, 98
Grasshopper Gumbo, 52

Happy Birthday, Mother Dearest, 10
Hello! How Are You? I Am Fine!, 36

I Am a Ghost Who's Lost His Boo, 42
I Am Digging a Hole in the Ceiling, 86
I Am Growing a Glorious Garden, 12
I Am Sitting Here and Fishing, 112
I Am Tired of Being Little, 24
I Am Wunk, 20
I Did Not Eat Your Ice Cream, 125
I Know All the Sounds that the Animals Make, 9
I Lost My Invisible Puppy, 132
I'm Certain I Sing Like an Angel, 141

I Met a Rat of Culture, 38
I'm Much Too Tired to Play Tonight, 115
I'm Off to Catch a Bumblebee, 84
I'm Sorry!, 93
I Saw a Brontosaurus, 138
I Should Have Stayed in Bed Today, 28
I Want a Pet Porcupine, Mother, 120
I Wave Good-bye When Butter Flies, 80
I Wish My Father Wouldn't Try to Fix Things Anymore, 102

Katy Ate a Baked Potato, 59
Kevin the King of the Jungle, 30

Last Night I Dreamed of Chickens, 44
Life's Not Been the Same in My Family, 37
Little Bird Outside My Window, 32

Mold, Mold, 122
Moodles Have No Middles, The, 127
Mosquitoes, Mosquitoes!, 136
Mother Goblin's Lullaby, 150
My Brother Built a Robot, 46
My Brother Is a Quarterback, 118
My Brother Is as Generous as Anyone Could Be, 130
My Brother's Bug, 151
My Family's Sleeping Late Today, 124
My Fish Can Ride a Bicycle, 146
My Frog Is a Frog, 82
My Mother Made a Meat Loaf, 66
My Neighbor's Dog Is Purple, 41
My Sister Ate an Orange, 147
My Snake, 116
My Uncle Looked Me in the Eye, 50
My Woolen Sweater Itches Me, 114
My Younger Brother's Appetite, 92

Nigel Gline, 76

Picklepuss Pearl, 129

Rains in Little Dribbles, The, 53
Remarkable Adventure, A, 56
Rhododendra Rosenbloom, 140

Sir Bottomwide, 126
Slow Sloth's Slow Song, 65
Smoking Yokadokas, The, 134
Something Big Has Been Here, 7
Spider, The, 88
Squirrels, 58
Super Samson Simpson, 143

There's a Worm in My Apple, 106
There's No One as Slow as Slomona, 74
They Never Send Sam to the Store Anymore, 78
They Tell Me I'm Peculiar, 27
Today I'm Going Yesterday, 72
Today I Shall Powder My Elephant's Ears, 54
Try Never to Tickle the Twickles, 108
Turkey Shot out of the Oven, The, 18
Twaddletalk Tuck, 64

Unhappy South Pole Penguin, 33

Warteena Weere Just Bit My Ear, 110
Watson Watts, 34
We Moved About a Week Ago, 94
We're Fearless Flying Hotdogs, 152
We're Four Ferocious Tigers, 11
We're Know-nothing Neebies, 68
Who Pulled the Plug in My Ant Farm?, 70
Why Do I Water My Flowers?, 142
Wilhelmina Wafflewitz, 83
Wumpaloons, Which Never Were, The, 145

You're Eating Like a Pig Again!, 23
You're Nasty and You're Loud, 26

Zoo Was in an Uproar, The, 62

Index to First Lines

A goat wandered into a junkyard, 98
An auk in flight, 48
An early worm got out of bed, 8
An elephant is hard to hide, 148
As soon as Fred gets out of bed, 14
As soon as Penny goes to bed, 144

Bats have shiny leather wings, 89
Belinda Blue was furious, 16
Benita Beane, the trumpet queen, 104

Denson Dumm, with pomp and flair, 22
Do not disturb the woolly Wurbbe, 40
Don't yell at me!, 75

Fenton Phlantz is fairly weird, 49
Four vain and ancient tortoises, 96
Fuzzy, you are underfoot!, 111

Go to sleep, my baby goblin, 150
Grasshopper Gumbo, 52

Happy birthday, Mother dearest, 10
Hello! How are you? I am fine!, 36

I am a ghost who's lost his boo, 42
I.......am.......a.......sloth......., 65
I am digging a hole in the ceiling, 86
I am growing a glorious garden, 12
I am sitting here and fishing, 112
I am Super Samson Simpson, 143
I am tired of being little, 24
I am Wunk, a wacky wizard, 20
I did not eat your ice cream, 125
I know all the sounds that the animals make, 9
I lost my invisible puppy, 132
I'm Captain Conniption, 90
I'm certain I sing like an angel, 141
I met a rat of culture, 38
I'm Kevin the king of the jungle, 30

I'm much too tired to play tonight, 115
I'm off to catch a bumblebee, 84
I'm Picklepuss Pearl, and I'm not very nice, 129
I'm sorry I squashed a banana in bed, 93
I'm the barber of Shrubbery Hollow, 128
I'm the Disputatious Deeble, 100
I'm Twaddletalk Tuck and I talk and I talk, 64
I'm Wilhelmina Wafflewitz, 83
I saw a brontosaurus, 138
I should have stayed in bed today, 28
"I want a pet porcupine, Mother!," 120
I was at my bedroom table, 56
I wave good-bye when butter flies, 80

Katy ate a baked potato, strolling through the mews, 59

Last night I dreamed of chickens, 44
Life's not been the same in my family, 37
Little bird outside my window, 32

Mold, mold, 122
Mosquitoes, mosquitoes, 136
My brother built a robot, 46
My brother is a quarterback, 118
My brother is as generous, 130
My brother's bug was green and plump, 151
My family's sleeping late today, 124
My father's listed everything, 102
My fish can ride a bicycle, 146
My frog is a frog that is hopelessly hoarse, 82
My mother made a meat loaf, 66
My neighbor's dog is purple, 41
My sister ate an orange, 147
My snake, a long and limber pet, 116
My uncle looked me in the eye, 50
My woolen sweater itches me, 114
My younger brother's appetite, 92

Rhododendra Rosenbloom, 140

Sir Bottomwide, a stalwart knight, 126
Something big has been here, 7
Squirrels, often found in parks, 58

The Addle-pated Paddlepuss, 60
The day they sent Sam to the grocery store, 78
The Fuddies fly above the dale, 105
The Moodles have no middles, 127
The rains in Little Dribbles, 53
The spider, sly and talented, 88
The turkey shot out of the oven, 18
The Wumpaloons, which never were, 145
The zoo was in an uproar, 62
There's a worm in my apple, 106
There's no one as slow as Slomona, 74
They tell me I'm peculiar, 27
Today I'm going yesterday, 72
Today I shall powder my elephant's ears, 54
Try never to tickle the Twickles, 108

Unhappy South Pole penguin, 33

Warteena Weere just bit my ear, 110
Watson Watts, atop his head, 34
We moved about a week ago, 94
We're fearless flying hotdogs, 152
We're four ferocious tigers, 11
We're Know-nothing Neebies, 68
We're the Smoking Yokadokas, 134
When Nigel Gline sat down to dine, 76
Who pulled the plug in my ant farm?, 70
Why do I water my flowers?, 142

"You're eating like a pig again!," 23
You're nasty and you're loud, 26

OTHER BOOKS BY JACK PRELUTSKY

The Baby Uggs Are Hatching
Beneath a Blue Umbrella
The Headless Horseman Rides Tonight
It's Christmas
It's Halloween
It's Snowing! It's Snowing!
It's Thanksgiving
It's Valentine's Day
The Mean Old Mean Hyena
My Parents Think I'm Sleeping
The New Kid on the Block
Nightmares
The Queen of Eene
Rainy Rainy Saturday
Ride a Purple Pelican
Rolling Harvey Down the Hill
The Sheriff of Rottenshot
The Snopp on the Sidewalk
Tyrannosaurus Was a Beast
What I Did Last Summer
The Wild Baby by Barbro Lindgren (*translation*)
The Wild Baby Gets a Puppy by Barbro Lindgren (*translation*)
The Wild Baby Goes to Sea by Barbro Lindgren (*translation*)
Zoo Doings